Rocks & Minerals

of the
Pacific Coast

T0166282

Dan R. Lynch
& Bob Lynch

Adventure Quick Guides
YOUR WAY TO EASILY IDENTIFY ROCKS & MINERALS

Adventure Quick Guides

This guide covers 52 of the most common and collectible rocks and minerals on the Pacific Coast and will teach you simple guidelines for identifying them, as well as how to tell similar materials apart from each other. Guidelines are also included to help you recognize how weathering and other external forces can make a find look different than it "should."

Helpful notes for using this Quick Guide:

- Read the "How to Use This Guide" section carefully, as it will help novices learn the difference between a rock and a mineral

- The guidelines presented on the following pages consist of the basic knowledge all collectors will need to identify rocks and minerals

- This Quick Guide will work best as a supplement to a more in-depth field guide that covers the specific state or area in which you plan to collect

ROCKS & MINERALS GUIDES

For more information about rocks and minerals across your entire state, pick up the state-specific guides that discuss common, desirable, and rare finds accessible to collectors. Complete with full-color photographs that represent the specimens exactly as they appear in real life and with easy-to-use formats, these Adventure Publications titles are available from all major booksellers.

DAN R. LYNCH & BOB LYNCH

Dan R. Lynch grew up learning the subtle differences between rocks and the nuances of mineral identification first-hand in his parents' rock shop.
Bob Lynch, with wife Nancy, opened that rock shop in 1992, putting to work his stone cutting and polishing skills learned from a lifetime of being a jeweler. Together, Dan and Bob write a series of field guides to help readers "decode" the complexities of geology and figure out what exactly they've found.

10 9 8 7 6 5 4
Rocks & Minerals of the Pacific Coast
Copyright © 2018 by Dan R. Lynch
Published by Adventure Publications
An imprint of AdventureKEEN
310 Garfield Street South
Cambridge, Minnesota 55008
(800) 678-7006
www.adventurepublications.net
All rights reserved
Printed in China
ISBN 978-1-59193-775-3

Cover design by Jonathan Norberg
Book design by Dan R. Lynch

All photos by Dan R. Lynch
All images copyrighted

How to Use This Guide

If you are new to rock and mineral collecting, or are just a curious traveler wondering about the rocks underfoot, you may not know that every rock and mineral has distinctive identifying traits. Often, determining the identity of a rock or mineral is as simple as trying to scratch it with a pocket knife or noting how "shiny" it is. And once you've identified what you've collected, you've taken the first step toward being a collector, also known as a "rockhound." This book will teach you the identifying traits of 52 Pacific Coast collectibles.

What is the difference between rocks and minerals?
Rocks and minerals are intimately related yet quite different. **Minerals** can be thought of as a pure substance and consist of a definite chemical compound. Common table salt, for example, is actually a mineral called halite, which always consists of a chemical compound called sodium chloride. Because of their uniform compositions, minerals **crystallize**, or harden, into very definite shapes. Halite virtually always forms as perfect cubes. **Rocks**, on the other hand, contain a mixture of different minerals. Rocks form in a number of different ways—such as from the cooling of molten rock—but they always appear as masses consisting of grain-like mineral particles, whether the grains are large or microscopic.

A crystal of calcite, a mineral

A sample of gabbro, a rock

How do I identify a rock?
Studying rocks can get very complicated, and identifying rarer rock types will require you to do lots of research. But the most basic and abundant kinds of rock can be identified by noting hardness, color, texture, and grain size. A rock's **hardness** can vary, but whether or not a pocket knife will easily scratch a rock will aid in identification. One of the best traits to examine is **grain size**, which is a measure of the size of the mineral grains of which the rock is composed. Granite is an example of a coarse-grained rock, with large, chunky, easily visible mineral grains. And rhyolite is an example of a very fine-grained rock, with mineral grains so small that the rock appears uniform in color. Geologically, grain size is generally only used to describe volcanic rocks (formed from the solidification of molten rock), but for the purposes of this book, it will be used to describe the texture of all rocks.

Granite, a coarse-grained rock (actual size)

Diabase, a medium-grained rock (actual size)

Rhyolite, a fine-grained rock (actual size)

How do I identify a mineral?

With thousands of known minerals, telling one apart from another can be daunting. But unlike rocks, minerals have definitive features that are easy to test and examine. Only a handful of minerals are truly considered "common" and easily found by amateurs. To identify these, hardness, color, luster, and crystal shape are very helpful traits to note. The **hardness** of a mineral can be determined by scratching it with a tool, such as a pocket knife, or against your fingernail. When trying to scratch a mineral, it is important to not apply too much pressure, as this can give you a false result. The tool must easily "bite" into the mineral without high pressure. **Luster**, a measure of how "shiny" a mineral is, is also very helpful to note. For example, some minerals are dull, or barely shiny at all, while many are glassy, or glass-like. Many others are obviously metallic. But it is **crystal shape** that is the most important trait to examine. Minerals form in definitive shapes, so two specimens of the same mineral, even those from different sides of the Earth, will share the same shape. Being able to identify a particular mineral's shape is critical to determining its identity. The exception is when a specimen is broken or when it formed **massively** (with no crystal shape evident, such as when it formed in a tight space). In these cases, you'll have to rely on other characteristics.

A well-formed crystal of dull feldspar

A massive sample of metallic chalcopyrite

Identifying your find

The first step is to determine if you've found a rock or a mineral. Once you've figured that out, go to the appropriate section of the book and compare your rock or mineral to the photos and see if it matches the description that follows. If you're having a hard time distinguishing your find because two of the minerals look alike (like quartz and calcite), read the "how are they different" notes, as this will teach you practical ways to differentiate them. If you can't seem to find your specimen in the book, you may have found something more uncommon or just more unusual; see "Final Notes."

Is there anything that I can't collect?

Collecting anything in national parks, on Native American reservations, and in some state and national forests is illegal. In addition, you'll be trespassing if you collect on privately owned property, so always be aware of where you are collecting and what the rules are.

Washington, Oregon, and California have rules prohibiting the collecting of vertebrate fossils (fossils of animals with a backbone, such as fish and reptiles) due to their scientific importance. It is also illegal to collect Native American artifacts. Both types of these finds should be left alone and reported to authorities. Please familiarize yourself with and respect national, state, and local laws before collecting.

Geology of the Pacific Coast

The Pacific Coast is a fascinating region, due in large part to the many geological forces at work here. Tectonic plates, the enormous sheets of rock that underlie our world, shift, slide, and collide along these western shores, resulting in dramatic cliffs, seaside mountains, and even volcanoes. Washington's Puget Sound and neighboring areas were also home to glaciers during the past ice age, resulting in an enormous amount of "foreign" rock material that was pushed southward from Canada. The expansive cliffside beaches of Oregon and northern California are an impressive setting for hunting fossils that weathered out of the rock and the endless specimens transported by waves and currents. Lastly, southern California is home to a mix of rugged, coarse volcanic rocks, presenting an entirely different set of materials to hunt. As long as you're mindful of unstable cliffs, rushing currents, and rising tides, you'll find endless collecting opportunities.

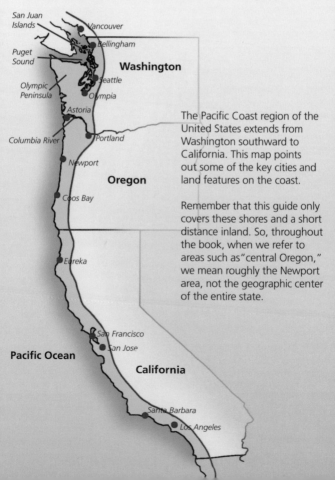

The Pacific Coast region of the United States extends from Washington southward to California. This map points out some of the key cities and land features on the coast.

Remember that this guide only covers these shores and a short distance inland. So, throughout the book, when we refer to areas such as "central Oregon," we mean roughly the Newport area, not the geographic center of the entire state.

Coarse-grained Rocks

Gabbro/Diabase
Fairly common dark, dense igneous rocks

- Hard; not typically scratched with a pocket knife
- Dark in color, usually black, brown, gray, or greenish; diabase tends to be lighter in color than gabbro
- Both are coarse, but gabbro has much larger grains; both can show embedded glassy rectangular crystals
- Somewhat common; look in far northwestern California and southwestern Oregon

 How are they different?
Gabbro and diabase are much darker in color than granite

Granite
A very common igneous rock that underlies North America

- Hard; not typically scratched with a pocket knife
- Dense and coarse-grained with mottled coloration; gray to black, yellow to brown, pink to reddish
- Contains large, angular mineral grains, some of which appear glassy or nearly metallic
- Very commonly found on any beach, but particularly in central and southern California

 How are they different?
Granite is more abundant and its light color grains are larger and more common

Diorite/Granodiorite
Uncommon igneous rocks that resemble granite

- Hard; not typically scratched with a pocket knife
- Dense and fairly coarse-grained with mottled coloration; usually black to gray and white
- Both kinds of rocks resemble granite, but with less variation in color; often appearing black and white
- Less common than most plutonic rocks in the region; found on Puget Sound and California beaches

 How are they different?
Andesite is usually finer-grained and is more dark gray in color

Andesite
A common volcanic rock typically found more inland

- Fairly hard; may be scratched with a pocket knife
- Fairly light in color; usually light to dark gray, often with light-colored grains or crystals throughout
- Dense and heavy, usually found in mountainous regions; often has embedded rectangular crystals
- Fairly common on the region's beaches, though usually found inland along the Cascade Mountains

Coarse- to medium-grained Rocks

Porphyry
Common rocks containing large, very conspicuous crystals

- Fairly hard; may be scratched with a pocket knife
- Resembles other rocks, such as basalt or andesite, but with large well-formed embedded crystals
- Crystals are often lighter colored and are conspicuous, appearing "out of place"
- Fairly common, with most coastal areas producing specimens; Puget Sound is a good place to look

 How are they different?
Porphyry contains crystals of a fairly uniform size and shape embedded in hard rock

Conglomerate and Breccia
Common rocks consisting of smaller rocks stuck together

- Both rocks vary greatly in hardness
- Conglomerate is a rock consisting of variously sized rounded stones cemented together
- Breccia is similar but consists of broken, angular rock fragments cemented together
- Both rocks are abundant in sedimentary-rich coastal areas, particularly northwest California

 How are they different?
Conglomerate and breccia are much coarser grained and more irregular

Greywacke *(pronounced "gray-wacky")*
A rock consisting of sand, silt, and clay hardened together

- Fairly soft; often scratched with a pocket knife
- Finer grained and somewhat even in color; usually gray to brown, often with white mineral veins
- Formed from sediments mixed up by water currents; feels gritty, with some visible grain size variation
- Quite common, found all over the Pacific Coast, particularly in Puget Sound and along central Oregon

 How are they different?
Greywacke is usually harder and darker in color; sandstone is very gritty and rough

Sandstone
A very common and widespread sedimentary rock

- Soft; can be scratched with a pocket knife
- Composed of cemented sand; coarse and gritty in texture, often easily freed of its sand grains
- Often light-colored in shades of brown to reddish; sometimes with darker colored layers within
- Extremely abundant all along the Pacific Coast, particularly on the Olympic Peninsula

Medium- to fine-grained Rocks

Gneiss *(pronounced "nice")*
A common metamorphic rock of varying composition

- Usually fairly hard; may be scratched with a pocket knife with some effort
- Vaguely layered with bands of varying coloration; it contains both coarser and finer mineral grains
- May resemble other rocks, particularly granite, but in a layered or banded form
- Common, found virtually anywhere along the coasts

How are they different?
Schist has much finer, more compact layers and often appears "glittery"

Schist
A common, dense, and highly layered metamorphic rock

- Often fairly hard; may be scratched with a pocket knife with some effort
- Dense and highly layered; typically gray to brown and may contain many tiny shiny mineral flecks
- Can contain embedded crystals of harder, collectible minerals within, such as garnet or amphiboles
- Abundant anywhere, especially on Oregon's coasts

How are they different?
Serpentinite does not have the tight layering of schist and tends to be dark green

Serpentinite
A metamorphic rock consisting of multiple serpentines

- Soft; can be scratched with a pocket knife
- Predominantly dark green in color, also with gray and brown; may have some layering
- Consists of various serpentine minerals, so it has their characteristic "greasy" look and feel
- Fairly uncommon but still collectible; look in southwest Oregon and in Puget Sound

How are they different?
Serpentinite is darker in color and somewhat harder; soapstone is more lustrous

Soapstone
An uncommon metamorphic rock consisting primarily of talc

- Very soft; easily scratched with a pocket knife
- Light-colored, usually in shades of green and tan to brown; often lustrous and shiny
- Consists of layered talc, chlorite, and amphiboles; "soapy" feeling, with lots of flakiness at edges
- Fairly scarce, but the central to southwestern Oregon and northwestern California coasts produce it

Fine-grained Rocks

Basalt
An abundant, dark, and dense volcanic rock

- Fairly hard; may be scratched with a pocket knife with some effort
- Very fine-grained and always dark in color; gray to black, but also greenish, or brown to reddish
- Very often contains bubble-like cavities, sometimes with mineral crystals growing within
- Common along the entire region

 How are they different?
Basalt is always darker colored than rhyolite; basalt doesn't usually have banding

Rhyolite
A fairly uncommon hard, fine-grained volcanic rock

- Very hard; can't be scratched with a pocket knife
- Finely grained and light-colored; often gray to brown or reddish
- May contain parallel bands of color, veins of minerals, or gas bubbles
- Less common than basalt but can be found in many places, particularly southern California

 How are they different?
Quartzite is glassier and translucent in thin pieces; rhyolite is coarser grained

Quartzite
A common, extremely hard and dense metamorphic rock

- Very hard; can't be scratched with a pocket knife
- Generally light in color, often with faint layering; typically translucent, especially at broken edges
- Grainy and glassy when freshly broken; smooth and dull when weathered
- Very abundant anywhere; central California and southwest Oregon have large deposits

Obsidian
Dark, translucent, and shiny volcanic glass

- Hard; not typically scratched with a pocket knife
- Very brittle, glassy, and dark colored, typically black but can be brown; translucent when thin
- Breaks into sharp-edged, semi-circular pieces; appears dull when weathered
- Rare along the beaches, but not unheard of; southwestern Oregon's rivers may produce pieces

Fine-grained Rocks

Limestone
Somewhat common, light-colored marine sedimentary rock

- Soft; can be scratched with a pocket knife
- Light-colored, sometimes with layers of varying coloration; has a dusty, gritty feel when broken
- Will "fizz" in strong vinegar and sometimes contains crystal-lined cavities
- Fairly common, found in many areas, particularly on the Olympic Peninsula and the San Juan Islands

 How are they different?
Limestone is harder and does not have the extensive layering seen in shale

Shale
An abundant, soft, highly layered sedimentary rock

- Soft; can be scratched with a pocket knife
- Fine-grained and very layered; layers often come apart easily, especially with a knife blade
- Fine-grained with typically even coloration, usually tan to brown; may contain fossils between layers
- Very common throughout the Pacific Coast region; the upper half of California's coast has much of it

 How are they different?
Shale and mudstone are very similar, but shale is highly layered; mudstone is not

Mudstone
A common, soft sedimentary rock with no layering

- Very soft; easily scratched with a pocket knife
- Resembles shale in most ways but is not layered
- Much like shale, mudstone is extremely fine-grained with even coloration, usually in shades of tan to brown, but also light to dark gray
- Abundant and found all along the Pacific Coast; common in Puget Sound and northwest California

 How are they different?
Clays are softer and very crumbly; clays also soften when wet; mudstone does not

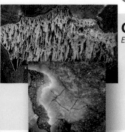

Clays
Extremely fine-grained mixtures of minerals and rock grains

- Very soft; easily scratched with your fingernails
- Composed largely of microscopic mineral grains; brittle when dry and sticky when wet
- Typically light-colored; tan to brown or gray is common, but can also be very white
- Clays are ubiquitous in all coastal areas; can be found in rock cavities in interesting forms

Dull to Glassy Minerals

Feldspar group
The most abundant mineral group, found in most rocks

- Hard; can't be scratched with a pocket knife
- Light-colored—white to gray, pink, or tan; typically opaque or very slightly translucent; dull to glassy
- Most commonly found as embedded grains in rocks like granite and andesite; frequently blocky and angular, but also as irregular masses
- Feldspars are extremely common in coastal rocks

> *How are they different?*
> Feldspars are much harder; calcite is not found as blocky grains within rocks

Calcite
A very common mineral, particularly in sedimentary rocks

- Soft; easily scratched with a pocket knife
- Light-colored (typically colorless to white), translucent, and often glassy; dull when weathered
- Forms crystals shaped as steep six-sided points or blocky "leaning" cubes; will "fizz" in vinegar
- Widespread and common, found anywhere there is limestone; Puget Sound is a lucrative area

> *How are they different?*
> Quartz is much harder than calcite; calcite breaks more readily

Quartz
The most common mineral, found nearly anywhere

- Very hard; can't be scratched with a pocket knife
- Light-colored, typically colorless to white or gray, glassy, and translucent to transparent
- Crystals have six sides and a pointed tip; masses are more common, often found as loose pebbles or embedded in rocks; brittle, breaks in circular patterns
- Quartz can be found literally anywhere on the coast

> *How are they different?*
> Beach glass is generally softer, uniform in thickness, and can be more colorful

Beach glass
Water-rounded glass that is frequently mistaken for quartz

- Hard; not easily scratched with a pocket knife
- Tends to be light-colored, colorless to white, but may be green, brown, blue, or red; translucent
- Broken glass becomes cloudy and dull when beach-worn; usually has a uniform thickness
- Beach glass is just manmade litter, but colorful pieces are popular and can be found anywhere

Dull to Glassy Minerals

Agate
Uncommon banded gemstones of mysterious formation

- Hard; can't be scratched with a pocket knife
- Color varies greatly; multicolored in concentric rings; usually white to gray, yellow to brown, red
- Found as waxy, rounded colorful pebbles; translucent when thin; breaks in circular shapes if struck
- Uncommon but very popular, agates are frequently found along central Oregon's coasts, near Newport

> *How are they different?*
> Chalcedony's color is often mottled, while agates are organized in ring-like bands

Chalcedony (pronounced "kal-sed-oh-nee")
A common variety of compact, dense quartz

- Hard; can't be scratched with a pocket knife
- Color can vary greatly, though grays, browns, and reds are most common; color is often mottled
- Usually found as loose, rounded pebbles; translucent and waxy if freshly broken, dull if weathered
- Abundant and frequently found in Puget Sound, along central Oregon's coasts, and northern Cali

> *How are they different?*
> Jasper is always more opaque in bright light; jasper can be found as larger masses

Jasper
The very common and colorful variety of chert

- Hard; can't be scratched with a pocket knife
- Found in many colors, though typically brown to reddish, often mottled; opaque unless very thin
- Forms as veins or pockets in rock; usually found as loose pebbles with waxy, smooth surfaces
- Extremely common all along the Pacific Coast, easily found virtually anywhere

> *How are they different?*
> Chert is generally less colorful and often forms in much larger masses

Chert
Actually considered a rock, chert is composed of quartz

- Hard; can't be scratched with a pocket knife
- Typically light gray to brown or black; always opaque, sometimes with colored layers
- Extremely fine-grained with a waxy appearance when weathered; breaks in semi-circular shapes
- Very abundant anywhere along the coast; any hard, waxy stone can first be assumed chert

Dull to Glassy Minerals

Pyroxene group
A common family of dark, glassy minerals found in rocks

- Fairly hard; may be scratched with a pocket knife
- Typically dark colored, brown to black, sometimes green; usually very glassy and opaque
- Crystals are blocky, normally only seen as grains embedded in dark rocks like gabbro and diabase
- The pyroxenes are very common within beach rocks, but are normally very small and easily overlooked

> *How are they different?*
> Telling them apart is difficult; as a basic rule, look for pyroxenes in darker rocks

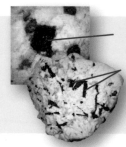

Amphibole group
Similar to the pyroxenes, this is a common family of minerals

- Fairly hard; may be scratched with a pocket knife
- Usually fairly dark colored (gray to brown) but sometimes white to tan; opaque
- Crystals tend to be elongated, normally seen within lighter-colored coarse rocks like granite
- Like the pyroxenes, amphiboles are very common within beach rocks, but normally go unnoticed

> *How are they different?*
> They're actually not; tremolite is an amphibole that can be found in larger masses

Tremolite/Actinolite
These amphibole minerals are scarce beach finds

- Fairly hard; may be scratched with a pocket knife
- Generally light-colored; white to brown, sometimes green to black; opaque, with a fibrous appearance
- These closely related amphiboles can be found as loose masses with a silky, flaky appearance
- It's fairly rare to find these in collectible masses, but Puget Sound and southwest Oregon yield specimens

> *How are they different?*
> Petrified wood is harder and doesn't have surfaces that are quite as flaky or fiber-like

Petrified wood
Actually fossilized wood, included here for comparison

- Ancient wood preserved as rock, often chert
- Hard; can't usually be scratched with a pocket knife
- Usually tan to brown in color, but may be darker
- Exhibits wood-like features, such as wood grain, bark, and even tree limbs
- Rare but collectible in many areas, particularly the coasts of central Oregon and central California

Dull to Glassy Minerals

Olivine
A hard mineral found in dark rocks or loose in sand

- Hard; can't be scratched with a pocket knife
- Typically yellow to yellow-green in color, also dark green to brown; glassy and translucent
- Rarely found crystallized; usually seen as glassy grains in dark rocks like gabbro, or loose in sand
- Very common, but usually only as tiny grains; yellow-green grains of sand are extremely abundant

 How are they different?
Epidote is more common as larger masses, usually as crusts rather than as grains

Epidote
A fairly uncommon but easily identified hard mineral

- Very hard; can't be scratched with a pocket knife
- Commonly yellow-green in color, but sometimes darker; crystals are translucent, crusts are not
- Normally seen as crusts or veins on or in rocks like granite or basalt; crystals are rare and usually tiny
- Fairly scarce on coastal beaches, most often found as yellow-green "stains" on dark rocks

 How are they different?
Jade is softer with a more waxy appearance; jade is often darker in color

Jade
A popular green gemstone collected for centuries

- Fairly hard; may be scratched with a pocket knife
- Light to dark green in color, sometimes mottled with brown or gray; usually with a "greasy" luster
- Found as loose water-worn pebbles, which may be translucent if thin
- Fairly rare, best found along California's northwestern and Oregon's southwestern coasts

 How are they different?
Jade is much harder and scarcer than serpentines

Serpentine group
This is a common family of soft, "slippery" minerals

- Soft; can be scratched with a pocket knife
- Serpentine minerals are typically green to yellow or brown in color; opaque and "greasy" in appearance
- Forms as irregular masses or veins; may be found as rounded pebbles that are "slippery" to the touch
- Less common on beaches than inland; can be found in southwest Oregon and on Puget Sound islands

Dull to Glassy Minerals

Chlorite group
Very common soft group of minerals found in cavities

- Very soft; easily scratched with your fingernail
- Dark-colored in shades of green or green-brown; opaque with a "greasy" luster
- Usually found as thin green coatings within cavities in dark rocks like basalt; often occur with zeolites
- Common, but easily overlooked; look in basalt-rich areas such as northwest Oregon

> **How are they different?**
> Celadonite is distinctively blue-green in color and can be found as larger masses

Celadonite
A very soft and often vividly colored cavity-filling mineral

- Very soft; easily scratched with your fingernail
- Usually light green to blue-green; opaque and chalky, sometimes with a "fuzzy" appearance
- Found as masses or coatings within cavities and gas bubbles in volcanic rocks, especially basalt
- Northern Oregon produces large masses; its conspicuous color makes it easy to spot in dark rocks

> **How are they different?**
> Talc is even softer and usually more lustrous; talc is more apple-green to brown

Talc
The softest mineral, found sparingly along the Pacific Coast

- Extremely soft; can be scratched with your fingernail with little effort
- Light-colored, usually pale green to gray, often with tan or brown outer surfaces; lustrous and flaky
- Forms as masses or veins that feel "slippery" or "soapy"; thin pieces may be translucent
- Fairly scarce; central Oregon produces small masses

> **How are they different?**
> Micas are far more common, especially within rocks; micas appear nearly metallic

Mica group
A family of flaky minerals common as a constituent of rocks

- Very soft; easily scratched with your fingernail
- Often dark-colored, gray to brown or black; often so shiny as to look almost metallic
- Forms as flaky stacks of thin, flexible crystals; typically seen as dark shiny spots in rocks like granite
- Micas are very common and found in many rocks; the lower half of California is a good place to look

Dull to Glassy Minerals

Garnet group
A very hard, fairly common, and popular mineral family

- Very hard; can't be scratched with a pocket knife
- Dark-colored, often red to brown; commonly translucent and glassy
- Crystals form as faceted "balls," often in gneiss or schist; tiny crystals and grains can be found in sand
- Garnets are common as tiny grains in beach sand; Puget Sound may be better for larger specimens

Garnet grain in sand; 4x actual size

> *How are they different?*
> Garnets are much more common; fluorapatite forms as tiny elongated crystals

Fluorapatite
A very rare and tiny collectible from the shore

- Fairly hard; may be scratched by a pocket knife
- Often colorless or white, but also yellow to green; glassy and translucent
- Forms as thin six-sided crystals, usually very small; found in sand with magnification and patience
- Very rare on the coast within its host rock; can be found in cavities in andesite, more common in sand

Crystal from sand; 5x actual size

> *How are they different?*
> Zeolites are more common and are usually found in cavities within rocks

Zeolite group
A fairly uncommon family of minerals that form in cavities

- Soft; can be easily scratched with a pocket knife
- Usually colorless to white, but sometimes yellow or pink; often glassy and translucent
- Zeolites form as tiny needle-like or angular crystals within cavities in dark rocks, particularly basalt
- Zeolites tend to be tiny and fragile, making them scarce, but they are abundant in northwest Oregon

> *How are they different?*
> Apophyllite is much rarer and tends to form in more square shapes with sharp points

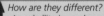

Apophyllite
A very rare mineral found inside volcanic rock cavities

- Soft; can be scratched by a pocket knife
- Almost always colorless to white; glassy and translucent, sometimes with a pearly sheen
- Forms blocky, square crystals with tapered points; often found in cavities in basalt with zeolites
- Rare near the coast, but found a bit farther inland in Oregon, along the Columbia River

Metallic Minerals

Hematite
An abundant iron-bearing mineral, found in many places

- Fairly hard; may be scratched with a pocket knife with some effort; often softer if formed as a crust
- Metallic-gray when well-formed; usually rusty red, opaque, and dusty when weathered
- Crystals aren't found on the shore; most abundant as reddish stains or crusts on or in rocks
- Very common anywhere; look for red-tinted rocks

Jasper stained red by hematite

How are they different?
Hematite turns reddish when crushed and powdered; goethite turns orange-brown

Goethite/Limonite *(pronounced "ger-tite")*
Common iron minerals found as yellowish crusts

- Fairly hard; can barely be scratched with a knife; softer when found as crusts or chalky masses
- Goethite is metallic black to brown; limonite (a mixture of goethite and other iron minerals) is a dusty, chalky yellow-brown to orange
- Crystals aren't found on the shore; both are common only as crusts or veins on or in rocks or clay

Goethite and limonite coatings on beach rocks

How are they different?
Goethite is not magnetic and will not attract a magnet; magnetite will

Magnetite
A common iron-bearing mineral that is strongly magnetic

- Fairly hard; not easily scratched by a pocket knife
- Black and metallic; will strongly attract a magnet
- Takes the form of octahedrons (crystals that resemble two pyramids placed bottom-to-bottom) or as irregular shiny-to-dull masses
- Very common as dark grains of sand on any beach (collect them with a magnet); rare in larger sizes

Crystal in sand; 4x actual size

How are they different?
Both are magnetic, but ilmenite will bond weakly and can be easily shaken free

Ilmenite
One of the most abundant titanium-bearing minerals

- Fairly hard; may be scratched with a pocket knife
- Metallic black, sometimes with a bluish tint
- Crystals are extremely rare; most easily found as magnetic blue-black metallic grains of sand
- The beaches near Astoria, Oregon, are so rich with ilmenite grains that mining them was once attempted; collect them with a magnet

Blue-black crystal grain in gabbro

Metallic Minerals & Misc.

Gold
A rare and highly sought-after precious metal

- Very soft; easy to scratch with a pocket knife
- Gold is always brightly metallic yellow
- Often found only as tiny flecks in sand; can also be found as tiny veins or flecks embedded in quartz
- Extremely rare and not usually found on coastal beaches, but tiny grains can be found up adjoining rivers in central and southern California

3x actual size

3x actual size

> **How are they different?**
> Pyrite is harder, brittle, brassy in color, and much more common

Pyrite
"Fool's gold" is one of the most common metallic minerals

- Very hard; can't be scratched with a pocket knife
- Brassy yellow in color and usually very brightly metallic, unless coated in limonite
- Develops as cube-shaped crystals that are often embedded in rocks; also as irregular masses or veins
- Fairly common in sedimentary rocks all along the coast; northwest California will produce pieces

Animal fossils
Preserved remains of ancient animal life

- Traces of animals, particularly clams, snails, mussels, scallops, and coral, embedded in rock
- Most fossils are found in between the layers in shale, or in limestone or sandstone
- Fossils are often fairly soft and are very similarly colored as the rock they are embedded within
- May be found all along the coast; central Oregon produces shellfish embedded in sandstone

Petrified wood in beach sand

Plant fossils
Remains of ancient plant matter preserved in rock

- Impressions of plants, especially leaves, twigs, and ferns, embedded in rock
- Most plant fossils are found in the layers of shale
- Plant fossils are normally very thin and colored very similarly to their host rock
- Rarer than animal fossils; northern Puget Sound produces nice specimens, and petrified wood can be found on central Oregon's beaches

Miscellaneous

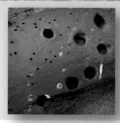

Boreholes
Clean-cut circular tubes in rocks

- Round, often perfectly circular holes that appear to be cut into rocks; these are made by burrowing mollusks, which cut a tunnel into rock
- The rocks are usually softer sedimentary types, such as shale, Greywacke, and sandstone
- Commonly seen in boulders anywhere along the coast during low tide

How are they different?
Boreholes tend to be sharp, straight "tubes;" concretion holes are irregular

Concretions
Conspicuously spherical rock formations

- Nearly perfectly round, hardened sedimentary rock "balls," softer than most rounded beach rock
- Concretions weather out of sedimentary rocks like sandstone and shale; most are tan to brown
- When they weather out of rock, they leave behind irregular honeycomb-like holes
- Uncommon in Puget Sound and northern California

Mineral veins
Stripes and lines of color crisscrossing beach rocks

- Thin veins of minerals that formed within the cracks and fissures in rocks as they weathered
- May be many colors; black (often manganese minerals) and red or yellow (iron minerals) are common
- Common host rocks are chert and Greywacke
- Very common on any beach, especially in Puget Sound and the San Juan Islands

Seashell fragments
Shells of sea creatures; included here for comparison

- Most seashells are clearly organic, but broken and worn fragments can be striped and resemble minerals like agate
- Seashells are softer than most similar-looking rocks and minerals, and will slowly dissolve in vinegar
- Seashells are extremely abundant and can be found all along the Pacific Coast; some local towns encourage collecting them

Final Notes

I can't find my specimen in the book. Does that mean it's rare?
Not likely. There are many rocks and minerals that are considered "common"; the types represented here are simply among the most abundant. In fact, perhaps as much as 90 percent of what a beginning collector will easily find is presented in this guide. So while you may have found something a bit more uncommon than most rocks or minerals, it is more likely that weathering or staining has altered the appearance or hardness of your common specimen and it no longer appears quite as you would expect it to.

The Pacific Coast region is particularly harsh on rocks and minerals, and millennia of mechanical and chemical weathering has sometimes dramatically changed the appearance of otherwise common materials. An example of this are the "mineral veins" shown on the previous page. In addition, the appearance of a given rock or mineral can vary greatly; basalt, for example, can be bluish-gray, greenish, reddish, or black, depending upon the conditions in which it formed. Additionally, ancient glaciers and wave action have carried "foreign" materials far from where they originally formed. For that reason, many less common materials, especially rocks, are not included in this book; identifying these rarer materials usually requires more experience or the aid of a microscope or other equipment. So if you really think you've found something truly rare, you may have; your next step will be further research, noting where you found it, its hardness, color, etc., and perhaps even seeking professional help from a geologist at a school or museum. But try to keep wishful thinking from clouding the identification process.

What equipment is helpful to bring?
If you're planning on just walking along the beach, then you won't need much more than a bucket or a backpack to carry your finds, though a camera and a magnifying lens are useful. If you're planning to dig and break rock, however, you'll need thick, sturdy leather gloves, a rock hammer (not a nail hammer), and eye protection, as well as digging implements. Tissues or paper towels are great to protect any fragile specimens. And always stay safe: Remember to bring water, a compass or GPS, and a cell phone along with you.

Glossary

Band: An easily identified layer of a differing color within a rock or mineral

Crystal: A solid body with a repeating atomic structure formed when an element or chemical compound solidifies

Facet: An angular side or face of a crystal

Igneous rock: Rock formed from the cooling and solidification of molten rock material originating from beneath the Earth's crust

Mass: A mineral formation lacking an obvious crystal shape

Metamorphic rock: Rock formed from the heating and/or compression of older rocks; metamorphic rocks often exhibit layered or warped features

Mineral: A naturally occurring chemical compound or native element that solidifies with a definite internal crystal structure

Octahedron: A three-dimensional structure with eight faces, resembling two pyramids placed base-to-base

Rock: A massive aggregate of mineral grains

Sedimentary rock: Rock formed when sediment is cemented together; a region in which sedimentary rocks are predominant is referred to as sedimentary

Vein: A mineral, often a metal, that has filled a crack or similar opening in a host rock or mineral

Volcanic rock: Rock formed by the cooling and solidification of molten rock erupted on or near the Earth's surface; see *igneous rock*

Widespread: Found in many places, though not necessarily abundant or common

Recommended Reading

Bonewitz, Ronald Louis. *Smithsonian Rock and Gem*. New York: DK Publishing, 2005.

Chesteman, Charles W. *The Audubon Society Field Guide to North American Rocks and Minerals*. New York: Knopf, 1979.

Lynch, Dan R., and Bob Lynch. *Rocks & Minerals of California (Quick Guide)*. Cambridge: Adventure Publications, 2017.

Lynch, Dan R., and Bob Lynch. *Rocks & Minerals of Washington and Oregon*. Cambridge: Adventure Publications, 2012.

Mottana, Annibale, et al. *Simon and Schuster's Guide to Rocks and Minerals*. New York: Simon and Schuster, 1978.

Pough, Frederick H. *Rocks and Minerals*. Boston: Houghton Mifflin, 1988.

Robinson, George W. *Minerals*. New York: Simon & Schuster, 1994.

Adventure Quick Guides

Only Rocks & Minerals Found on the Pacific Coast

Organized by rocks/minerals, then by appearance, for quick and easy identification

Simple and convenient—narrow your choices by group, and view just a few photos at a time

- Pocket-size format—easier than laminated foldouts
- Professional photos showing key traits
- Tips for identifying rocks and minerals
- "How are they different?" notes that contrast similar specimens

Improve your identification skills with this popular guide, journal, and playing cards

ISBN 978-1-59193-775-3 **$9.95**

5 0 9 9 5

9 781591 937753

PUBLICATIONS
Adventure
an imprint of AdventureKEEN

NATURE
ROCKS & MINERALS